Mini GROCERY STORE

BY THE EDITORS OF KLUTZ

KLUTZ®

WHAT YOU GET

BASICS

8 COLORS OF AIR-DRY CLAY

SUPER SOFT

CRAFTING ESSENTIALS

BEAD EYES

SEQUIN CHEEKS

GLAZE

SUPER SHINY

TRAY

NEW ITEM!

PUNCH-OUT DECORATIONS

Farm Fruits GRAPE JELLY

ORANGE Juice

Strawberry PRESERVES

100% Cute of FRUIT

EXTRAS

SHOPPING BASKET

SPECIAL BRAD DETAIL

PIZZA BOX

SUPER SHAPERS

DOUBLE-TIPPED CLAY TOOL

Carton

CARTON AND JAR FORMS

Jar

CLAY ROLLER

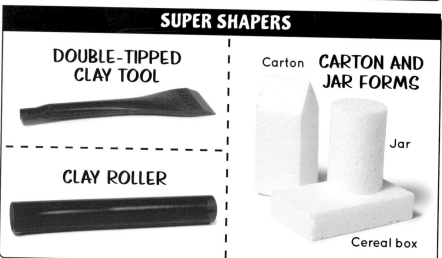

Cereal box

GATHER UP THESE THINGS FROM YOUR KITCHEN:

- Toothpicks
- Wax paper
- Storage baggies

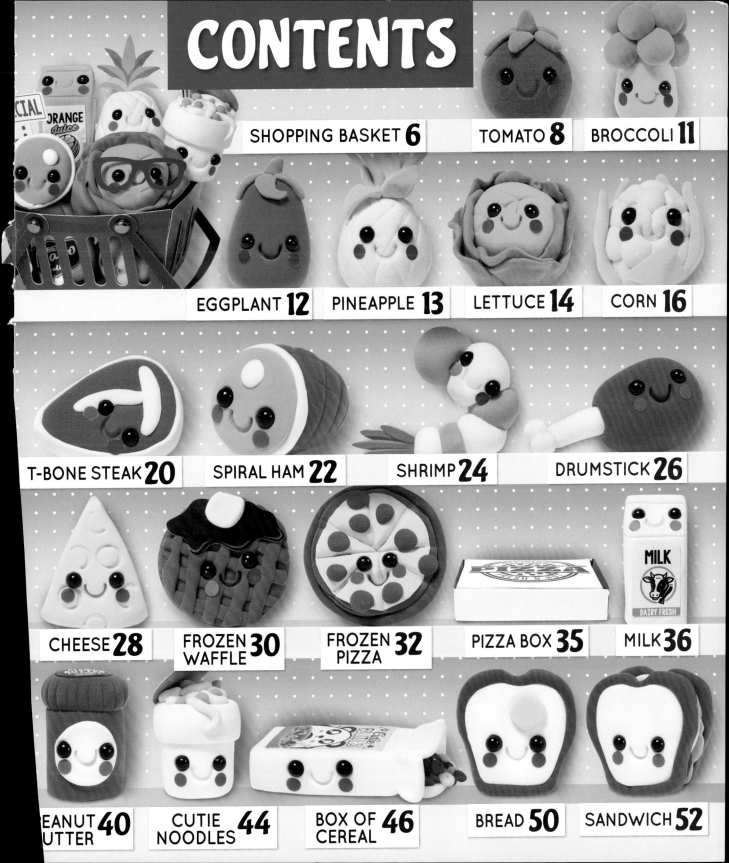

CONTENTS

CLAY BASICS

Read these tips to help you set up your work station and craft using the tools and materials in this book.

Prep WORK

- Cover your work surface with a sheet of wax paper or foil to protect your table. Clay is messy!

- Keep toothpicks and a damp paper towel handy. True coupon clippers always want to be prepped for a messy grocery store.

AIR-DRY Clay

- Most projects will firm up in 30 minutes. However, it's best to wait overnight for the clay to fully dry before you let other people hold them.

- Keep unused clay in an air-tight storage baggie after you open it. It will dry up if left out too long.

- If you forget to put the clay away, add a small amount of water to it. Massage and squeeze the wet clay until it feels soft again.

- You can make any of the recipes in this book with air-dry clay from your local arts-and-craft store.

- Smoosh the clay to make it softer. Let the clay rest for a few minutes to make the clay harder.

USING Glaze

- Use the glaze any time you want the clay to look shiny, or use it to glue things to the clay.

- Remember to put the glaze cap back on the bottle so that the glaze doesn't dry up.

- After using the glaze a couple times, you may want to wipe the brush with a damp paper towel. This way you will get a smooth coat every time.

- If you get any glaze on your hands or work surface, simply wash it off with warm soapy water.

Remember

Wash your hands after crafting.

These projects are super cute, but they are not toys. Keep finished projects and crafting supplies away from babies and pets.

Keep your craft supplies away from real food and kitchen supplies.

Don't eat items from this grocery even if they look tasty. They are NOT food.

MAKE A BALL

To make a big ball of clay, tear off a bit about the size you want it to be. Roll the clay between your palms in a circular motion until it's nice and round.

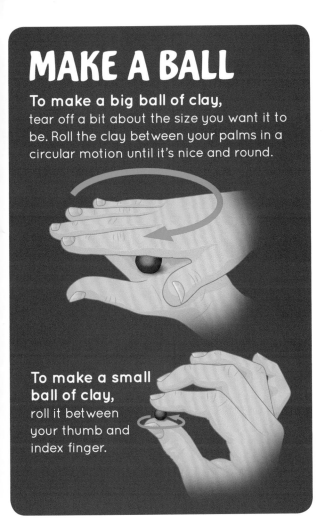

To make a small ball of clay, roll it between your thumb and index finger.

MEASURING CLAY

At the beginning of each project, there is a chart that shows how many balls of clay you need and how big each ball should be.

Make a clay ball this big:	Flatten the clay ball this big:
◯	◯

After you've rolled each ball, sit it on top of the chart to make sure you've got the right size. Don't roll inside the book because the clay may stick to the pages.

- - - - - - - - - - - - - - - - - - -

- If the ball is too small, add a bit of clay and roll the ball until it's smooth.

- If the ball is too big, pinch off a bit of clay and roll it again. Remember to put your scraps back into an air-tight baggie to use later!

USING THE CLAY TOOLS

Use this end to add a mouth and texture.

Use this end to cut the clay.

Use this tool to roll the clay flat.

SHOPPING BASKET

You'll Need:

SHOPPING BASKET AND HANDLES

4 METAL BRADS

GLUE OR CLEAR TAPE FROM HOME

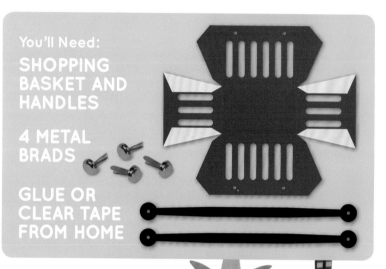

1 Place the side with the gray triangles facing up, then fold up the two side panels. Fold in all four tabs.

2 Fold the ends up and glue the tabs to the gray triangles.

3 Use four brads to attach the handles to the basket. Separate the brad's ends to hold them in place.

Fresh PRODUCE QUALITY

START YOUR SHOPPING SPREE WITH TOO-CUTE FRUITS AND A VARIETY OF VEGGIES.

Juicy TOMATO

PREMIUM
Finest
PRODUCE
Quality
TOP GRADE

TOMATO BODY
Make a clay ball this big:

1 Roll a tomato body.

LEAVES
Make 5 clay balls this big:

Make each into a coil this long:

MAKE LEAVES

2 Roll the leaves into short coils.

3 Pinch one end of each leaf thinner so that it makes a point.

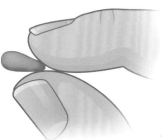

MAKE A COIL

Lay a ball on your work surface and use your pointer finger to roll it back and forth. The ball will turn into a rope.

To make the same thickness from end to end, use even pressure and roll your fingers over different parts of the tube as it gets longer.

4 Place one of the leaves on the body. Use your finger to flatten the leaf slightly.

5 Add the other four leaves in a circle, with the pointy ends on the outside. Leave a small open space in the middle of the circle of leaves.

SHOPPER'S TIP
You can also use the included paper leaf instead of making the leaves out of clay. Use glaze to attach it to the top of the tomato.

MAKE A STEM

6 Roll the stem into a very short coil. Press one end into the center of the leaves.

STEM
Make a clay ball this big:

Make a coil this long:

If you want to add a face, follow the directions on the next page.

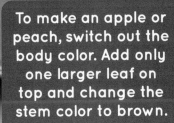

To make an apple or peach, switch out the body color. Add only one larger leaf on top and change the stem color to brown.

MAKE A FACE

Give your grocery gang personalities!

1 Use the notched end of the tool to make a mouth.

It's easiest to make the mouth first so you can use it as a guide to line up the eyes and cheeks.

PLEASANT PRODUCE

Hold the tool so the notch curves up to make a smile.

GRUMPY GROCERIES

Flip the notch upside down to make a frown.

2 To add a pair of eyes, dab a dot of glaze on either side of the mouth. Then stick the flat side of the black bead eyes to the glaze dots.

You can also use paper leaves instead of making them out of clay.

3 To add cheeks, use a dab of glaze under each eye. Then stick pink sequin cheeks to the glaze dots.

SEQUIN TIP:

Dip the tip of a toothpick in glaze to make a great sequin picker-upper tool.

Use the glaze to add paper accessories and leaves.

BROCCOLI

I'M Fresh

STEM

Make a clay ball this big:

1 Shape the stem into a cylinder by rolling it on its side.

2 Use your finger to roll on only one half of the stem so that end becomes slightly thinner.

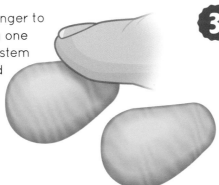

3 Stand the stem with the thinner end pointing up. Push down on it lightly so that the bottom flattens and widens slightly.

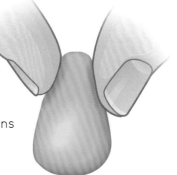

ADD THE FLORETS

FLORETS
Make 10 clay balls this big:

4 Lightly press the florets to the top of the stem.

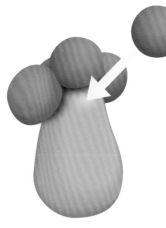

5 Add a face (see page 10).

EGGPLANT

BODY

Make a clay ball this big:

1. Follow Steps 1–3 on page 11 to shape the eggplant's body.

LEAVES

Make 5 clay balls this big:

LEAVES & STEM

2. Roll the leaves into short coils. Pinch one end of each coil thinner so that it makes a point.

3. Attach the leaves in a circle to the top of the eggplant body, with the pointy ends on the outside.

Leave a small open space in the middle of the circle of leaves.

4. Roll the stem into a very short coil. Press one end of the coil into the center of the leaves. This will be the eggplant stem.

STEM

Make a clay ball this big:

5. Add a face (see page 10).

PINEAPPLE

You can use paper pineapple leaves instead of clay.

1 Follow Steps 1–3 on page 11 to shape the pineapple's body.

BODY
Make a clay ball this big:

2 Press the straight edge of the tool into the pineapple's body at a diagonal angle. Press lines all the way around the pineapple at the same angle.

3 Turn the tool to create diagonal lines around the pineapple at the opposite angle.

ADD THE SPIKES

SPIKES
Make 9 clay balls this big:

4 Roll the leaves into short coils. Pinch one end of each coil thinner so that it makes a point.

Then, use your finger to flatten the coil into a flat leaf shape.

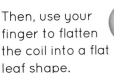

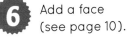

5 Attach the leaves to the top of the pineapple with the pointed ends facing up.

6 Add a face (see page 10).

Leafy LETTUCE

1 Use the straight edge of the tool to add some veins to the top of the core.

CORE
Make a clay ball this big:

USE THIS END OF THE TOOL:

ADD THE LEAVES

2 Use your finger to flatten each of the leaves into thin roundish shapes.

LEAVES
Make 8 clay balls this big:

Flatten ALL the leaves this big:

3 Add a leaf to the side of the core. Use your finger to smooth the bottom and sides of the leaf to the core. Do not smooth the top of the leaf.

4 Add the other leaves to the outside of the core. Overlap the leaves as you go and remember **NOT** to smooth down the top edges. Leave an open area on the top of the core.

5 Use your finger to smooth the bottom of the lettuce where all the leaves overlap.

6 Add a face (see page 10).

SHOPPER'S TIP

To make the lettuce look even more natural, gently bend the edges of the leaves outward with a toothpick before they dry.

To make a cabbage, change the leaves to purple and light green.

Try making a cauliflower by switching the core to white and the leaves to light green. Use the curved end of the tool to texture the top of the core.

CORN ON THE COB *Cutie*

COB
Make a clay ball this big:

KERNELS
Make 24 clay balls this big:

1 Follow Steps 1–3 on page 11 to shape the cob.

SHOPPER'S TIP
Make the kernels a few at a time as you add them to the body so that you do not have a bunch of tiny balls rolling everywhere.

2 Starting at the top, add the tiny yellow balls one at a time to the cob, and work your way down.

Try not to leave any gaps between the kernels.

3 You will run out of tiny balls before you reach the bottom of the body shape. This area will be covered by the husk leaves.

ADD THE HUSK

4 Roll the husk leaves into short coils. Pinch and roll each end of the coils to make them pointy.

Then, use your finger to flatten the coils into flat leaf shapes.

HUSKS
Make 5 clay balls this big:

Make each into a coil this long

5 Press one husk on the kernels, with one end tucked under the cob.

6 Add three more husks around the kernels.

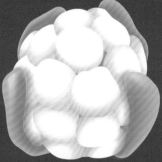

7 Press the last husk to the bottom of the cob. Fold the top over, away from the kernels.

8 Use your finger to smooth the bottom where all of the husks meet.

9 Add a face (see page 10).

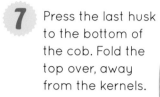

To make harvest corn, mix in red and orange kernels with the yellow.

SPECIAL

Meat MARKET

• MEDLEY •

MEET UP WITH THESE FRIENDLY
FACES DOWN AT THE MEAT COUNTER.

Tasty T-BONE STEAK

PREMIUM *Finest* **MEATS** *Quality* **TOP GRADE**

1 Follow Steps 1–3 on page 11 to shape the meat. Then place the shape on its side.

MEAT
Make a clay ball this big:

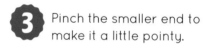

2 Use the palm of your hand to flatten the meat.

It should be about this size:

3 Pinch the smaller end to make it a little pointy.

ADD THE FAT

Make a clay ball this big: ● **Make a coil this long:**

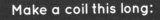

4 Roll the fat into a long coil.

5 Use the roller tool to gently flatten the coil into an even strip.

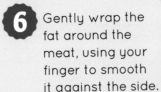

The strip should be about this wide after you flatten it.

6 Gently wrap the fat around the meat, using your finger to smooth it against the side.

If the strip is too short, gently pull the strip to stretch it longer.

If the strip is too long, just pinch off the extra clay.

ADD BONES

Make 2 clay balls this big: ● ● **Make 2 coils this long:**

SHOPPER'S TIP
For the perfect presentation, use plastic wrap from home to wrap your meats on the included tray. Make sure to let your project dry first.

7 Roll each bone into a short coil.

8 Place the two coils onto the steak in a T shape and smooth them down with your finger.

9 Add a face (see page 10).

MINI GROCERY **MEATS** HIGH QUALITY

Super
SPIRAL HAM

1 Follow Steps 1–2 on page 11 to shape the meat.

2 Set the meat upright with the wider end down. Holding it between your fingers, gently press so the bottom flattens quite a bit.

It should look like this:

MEAT
Make a clay ball this big:

CUT SIDE
Make 2 clay balls this big:

HOW TO MAKE PINK

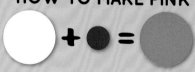

Squish the white and red balls together until the clay turns solid pink.

3 Flatten the pink cut side.

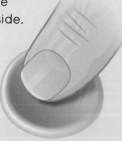

Flatten the clay ball this big:

4 Place the cut side onto the flat end of the meat. Use your finger to smooth the edge down.

5 Use the tool to make diagonal lines around the ham shape (see Steps 2–3 on page 13).

ADD THE FAT

| Make a clay ball this big: ⬤ |
| Make a coil this long: ▬▬▬▬▬▬▬▬▬▬▬ |

6 Roll the fat into a long coil.

7 Wrap the fat around the cut side.

ADD THE BONE

BONE
Make a clay ball this big: ⬤

8 Press the bone against the cut side until it flattens out.

9 Add a face (see page 10).

Savory SHRIMP

King of the shrimp ring!

1 To make the shrimp body, gently press all of the body balls together. Switch between orange and white, going from biggest to smallest.

2 Use your fingers to slightly squish the line of balls together.

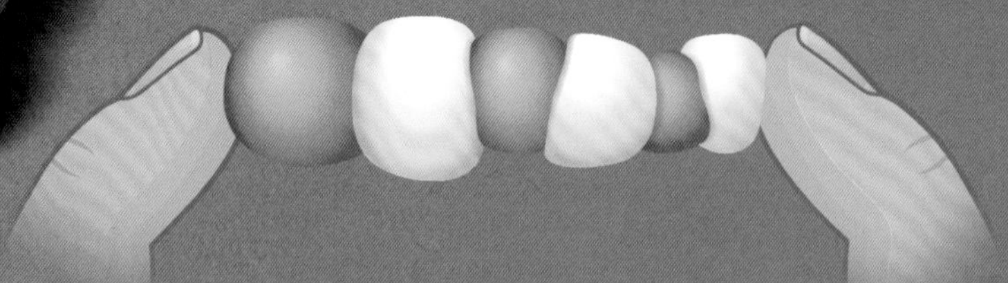

3 Gently roll the balls against your work surface so they really stick together.

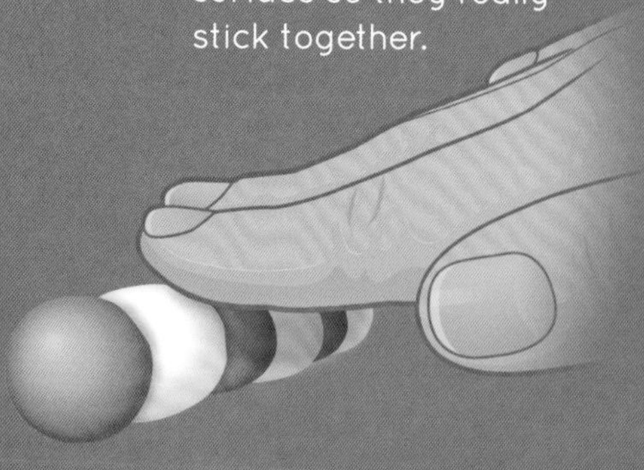

BODY
Make 6 clay balls in these sizes and colors:

TAIL
Paper punch-out

4 Bend the body into a curve.

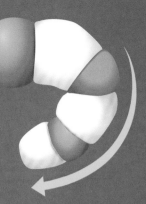

5 Stick the paper punch-out tail into the smaller end.

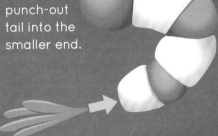

6 Add a face (see page 10).

(see page 10)

SHOPPER'S → *Secret*

THROW ANOTHER SHRIMP ON THE BARBIE!

KEBAB

Create your own kebab cuties by layering meats and veggies onto a bamboo skewer from home. It's easier to do this before your projects are totally dry.

DRUMSTICK

MEAT
Make a clay ball this big:

1 Follow Steps 1–2 on page 11 to shape the meat.

2 Poke the tool into the smaller end and twist it around a few times to create a small hole.

ADD THE BONE

Make a clay ball this big: Make a coil this long: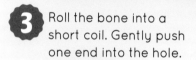

3 Roll the bone into a short coil. Gently push one end into the hole.

4 Press the two nubs onto the end of the bone.

NUBS
Make 2 clay balls this big:

5 Add a face (see page 10).

Cool FOODS

• FROZEN •

CHILL OUT IN THE
REFRIGERATOR AISLE WITH
THESE COOL CUTIES.

CHEESE WEDGE

CHEESE

Make a clay ball this big:

Flatten the clay ball this big:

1 Flatten the cheese with the palm of your hand.

2 Use the straight edge of the tool to cut two rounded sides off the cheese.

3 Set the cheese upright with the point up.

Gently press down on it so that the bottom edge flattens out and the cheese can stand on its own.

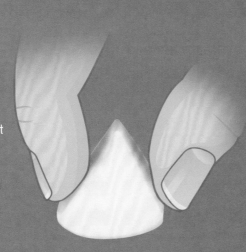

4 Use your finger to smooth any rough edges or wrinkles on the cheese.

5 Gently press the tool into the cheese surface to give it texture.

You can make full circles and half circles with the tool.

Don't forget the sides of the cheese.

Use orange clay for cheddar cheese.

6 Add a face (see page 10).

Try mixing yellow and orange clay to make a marbled cheese.

FROZEN WAFFLE

1 Flatten the batter with the palm of your hand.

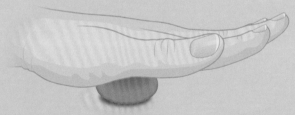

2 Roll each ridge into a coil.

BATTER
Make a clay ball this big:

Flatten the clay ball this big:

RIDGES
Make 10 clay balls this big:

Make each into a coil this long:

3 Place one ridge across the center of the waffle body.

4 Place two ridges on each side of the center ridge. Try to space them evenly.

Placing the center ridge first helps you evenly space out the others.

5 Place the other six ridges across the waffle in the opposite direction.

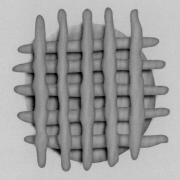

6 Flip the waffle over and use the straight edge of the tool to cut off any overhanging clay pieces.

7 Flip the waffle back over and use your finger to smooth down the ends of the ridges.

ADD THE TOPPINGS

You will need:
PAPER TOPPING

BUTTER
Make a clay ball this big:

Flatten the clay ball this big.

8 Use glaze to attach the paper punch-out topping to the waffle.

9 Flatten the butter. Then use the straight edge of the tool to flatten all four sides of the butter, forming a square.

10 Place the butter on top of the waffle and press lightly with your finger to attach.

11 Add a face (see page 10).

Use white glitter from home to frost the edges of your waffle.

FROZEN PIZZA

1 Flatten the dough with the palm of your hand.

DOUGH

Make a clay ball this big:

Flatten the clay ball this big:

MAKE THE CRUST

Make a clay ball this big:

2 Roll the crust into a long coil.

The coil should be this long.

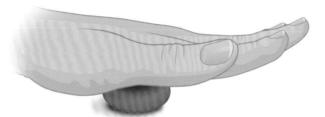

3 Wrap the crust around the dough.

If the coil is too short, gently pull the coil to stretch it longer.

If the coil is too long, just pinch off the extra clay.

SAUCE

Make a clay ball this big:

Flatten the clay ball this big:

CHEESE

Make a clay ball this big:

Flatten the clay ball this big:

PEPPERONI

Make 3 clay balls this big:

FOR MORE TOPPING IDEAS CHECK OUT THE NEXT PAGE.

ADD THE SAUCE

4 Place the flattened sauce on top of the dough. Use your finger to smooth it down.

ADD THE CHEESE

5 Place the flattened cheese on top of the sauce. Use your finger to smooth it down.

6 Gently press the tool into the top of the pizza to make a cut line. Press three more lines on the pizza to make slices. Don't cut all the way through!

ADD THE PEPPERONI

7 Separate each pepperoni ball into 3 tiny balls. Press them onto the pizza.

8 Add a face (see page 10).

SHOPPER'S TIP: You might want to leave an open area for the face.

OTHER TOPPINGS

Get creative with other pizza toppings. Check out the suggestions below or come up with your own ideas.

SLICED BELL PEPPER

Use the straight edge of the tool to cut a skinny green coil into short pieces.

SAUSAGE

Roll loose balls of brown clay and stick them onto the pizza. Use a toothpick to poke each ball multiple times to give it a sausage texture.

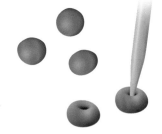

MUSHROOMS

Flatten small balls of white clay. Push the tool into the side to make a mushroom shape.

PIZZA BOX

Build your own paper pizza box that is just the right size for your cutie pie.

1 With the pizza box art facing down, fold the four small tabs up.

2 Fold the side flaps and front flap in.

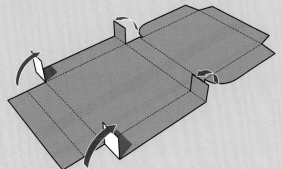

3 Fold the front flap over the small front tabs. Use glue or tape to help keep in place. Fold in the flaps on the lid.

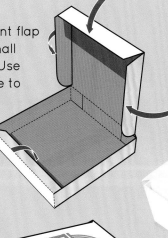

4 Close the lid, tucking the tabs into the box.

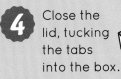

MILK

1 Roll the carton clay into a cylinder.

Use the palm of your hand to flatten the cylinder.

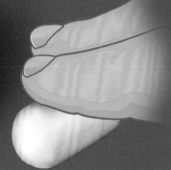

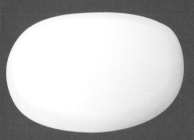

2 Use the roller to stretch the clay until it is long enough to wrap around the carton form.

The flattened clay should be this long:

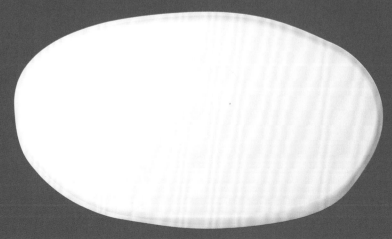

3 Lay the carton form in the center of the flattened clay.

4 Gently wrap the two long ends of the clay around the form.

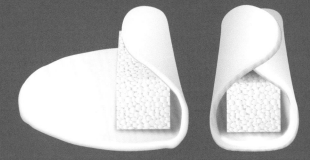

5 Carefully fold in the overhanging clay to cover the flat end.

6 To cover the pointy end of the form, gently pinch the clay closed at the top of the triangle.

7 Use your fingers to smooth and work the clay until the form is completely covered and looks flat all over.

BEFORE SMOOTHING

AFTER SMOOTHING

If any area gets too thick, just pinch off the extra clay.

8 Use the tool to lightly press two lines on either side of the pointy top edge. Press four more lines around the carton as shown.

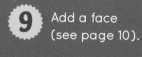

9 Add a face (see page 10).

Add a paper label to customize your carton. Learn how below.

Refresh your fridge by trying out a different carton color and adding paper labels to the front.

Brush some glaze on the front panel to attach a label to the carton.

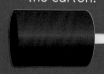

Fresh LEMONADE

Strawberry MILK

ORANGE Juice

Chocolate MILK

Fruity JUICE

Down THE AISLE

· STAPLES ·

NO SHOPPING TRIP IS COMPLETE
WITHOUT THESE SUPERMARKET STAPLES.

PEANUT BUTTER

1 Roll the peanut butter into a cylinder.

Use the palm of your hand to flatten the clay into a long shape.

2 Use the roller to stretch the clay until it is long enough to wrap around the form.

The flattened clay should be this long:

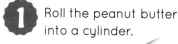

3 Lay the jar form in the center of the flattened clay.

4 Gently begin to cover the cylinder form by wrapping the two long ends of the clay around the form.

5 To cover one end of the cylinder form, gently fold in the overhanging clay.

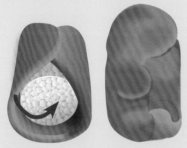

Cover the other end of the form in the same way.

6 Use your fingers to smooth and work the clay until the form is completely covered and does not look wrinkly.

If any area gets too thick, just pinch off the extra clay.

7 To finish smoothing and evening out the jar shape, use your fingers to roll the covered cylinder on its side.

The smoothed cylinder should look like this.

Turn the page to add my lid and label.

MAKE A LID

LID
Make a clay ball this big:

Flatten the clay ball this big.

8 Flatten the lid a little bit.

9 Place the lid on top of the covered jar and press lightly to attach.

10 Press the straight end of the tool into the side of the jar lid. Make small lines all the way around the lid.

ADD A LABEL

11 Use your finger to flatten out the label.

LABEL
Make a clay ball this big:

Flatten the clay ball this big.

12 Place the flattened label on the jar. Use your finger to smooth it down.

13 Add a face (see page 10).

To make peanut butter's best bud, swap out the brown color for purple and you've got a jolly jelly.

| STRAWBERRY JAM | MAYO | PICKLES | PASTA SAUCE |

| CHOCOLATE | GRAPE JUICE | SALSA |

SHOPPER'S Secret

You can create all kinds of canned cuties by changing up the color of the jars and adding different labels. Try making your own jar shapes.

| MUSTARD | KETCHUP | JELLY BEANS |

Cutie NOODLES

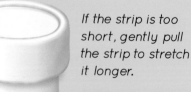

JAR FORM

Make a clay ball this big:

1 Follow Steps 1–7 on pages 40–41 to cover the jar form with the cup clay.

ADD BROTH

Make a clay ball this big:

Flatten the clay ball this big.

2 Use your finger to flatten the broth ball into a thin circle.

3 Press the broth circle onto the top of the cup to attach it.

ADD THE RIM

Make a clay ball this big:

Make a coil this long:

4 Roll the rim into a coil.

5 Use the roller to flatten the coil into an even strip.

6 Wrap the flattened rim around the top of the cup so that it sticks up above the broth a tiny bit.

If the strip is too short, gently pull the strip to stretch it longer.

If the strip is too long, just pinch off the extra clay.

MAKE NOODLES

NOODLE COLOR

○ + ● = ○

To make the light yellow noodle color, mix together the white and yellow clay balls.

7 Separate the noodle ball into **THREE** smaller balls and roll each one into a coil this long:

8 Loop and swirl each coil on top of the broth.

You can let some hang down over the edge.

ADD VEGGIES

You'll need spare scraps: ● ●

9 To make the peas and carrots, roll small scraps of orange and green clay into tiny balls and gently press them into the noodles.

You'll need: **PAPER LID**

10 Use a drop of glaze to attach the paper lid to one side of the noodle cup.

11 Add a face (see page 10).

BOX OF CEREAL

CEREAL BOX

Make a clay ball this big:

You will need:
BOX FORM

1 Roll the cereal box into a cylinder.

Use the palm of your hand to flatten the cylinder into a long shape.

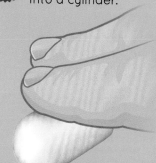

2 Use the roller to stretch the clay until it is long enough to wrap around the box form.

The flattened clay should be this long.

3 Lay the box form in the center of the flattened clay.

4 Gently begin to cover the box form by wrapping the two long ends of the clay around the form.

5 To cover one end of the box form, gently fold in the overhanging clay.

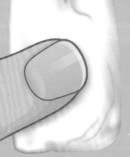

Cover the other end of the form in the same way.

6 Use your fingers to smooth and work the clay until the form is completely covered and looks smooth all over.

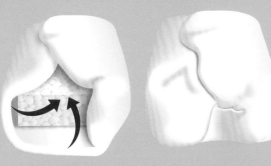

BEFORE SMOOTHING   *AFTER SMOOTHING*

If any area gets too thick, just pinch off the extra clay.

BOX FLAPS

Make 3 clay balls this big:

Roll each into a coil this long:

7 To make box flaps, roll each ball into a coil.

8 Use the roller very lightly to flatten the coils.

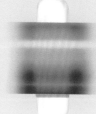

9 Use the straight edge of the tool to make neat rectangles.

10 Attach two of the flaps to the top and bottom edge of one end of the cereal box.

This will be the open end.

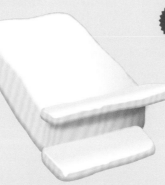

11 Use the straight edge of the tool to cut the last flap in half and attach each half to either side of the box end.

ADD THE CEREAL

12 To make the cereal, roll small scraps of different colors into tiny balls. Use a toothpick to poke a hole through the center of each cereal ball.

13 Fill the open end of the cereal box with pieces of cereal and have some spilling out.

14 Add a face (see page 10).

CEREAL VARIATIONS

Get creative with other types of cereal. Check out the suggestions below or come up with your own ideas.

COCO LOCOS

Roll small scraps of brown into tiny balls.

TOASTY OATS

Roll small scraps of brown into tiny balls. Use a toothpick to poke a hole in the center of each cereal ball.

CORN FLAKES

Tear off small bits of yellow clay.

SLICED BREAD

BREAD

Make a clay ball this big:

Flatten the clay ball this big:

1 Flatten the bread with the palm of your hand.

2 Use the tool to flatten all four sides of the bread, forming a square.

It should look like this.

ADD THE CRUST

Make a clay ball this big:

Make a coil this long:

3 Roll the crust into a coil.

4 Gently use the roller to flatten the coil into an even strip.

The strip should be about this wide after you flatten it.

5 Gently wrap the crust strip around the bread. Use your finger to smooth it against the side.

If the strip is too short, gently pull the strip to stretch it longer.

If the strip is too long, just pinch off the extra clay.

6 Use your fingers to gently squish the lower half of the bread slice to make it thinner.

7 Use the rounded end of the tool to dent the center of the top.

8 Add a face (see page 10).

Follow Step 9 on page 31 to make a square of butter. Press lightly to attach.

Make a clay ball this big:

Flatten the clay ball this big.

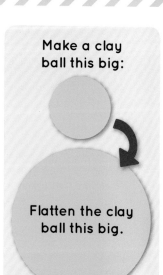

MAKE A SANDWICH

LETTUCE

1 Flatten the lettuce and make wrinkles as you lay it across the sliced bread.

TOMATO

2 Flatten the tomato balls and place them gently on top of the lettuce.

Make 3 clay balls this big:

Flatten the clay balls this big:

CHEESE

3 Flatten the cheese ball and use the tool to flatten all four sides of the cheese. Place it on top of the tomatoes.

 Make a clay ball this big:

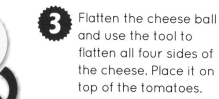

Flatten the clay ball this big.

4 Add another finished slice of bread to the top of the stack and add a face (see page 10).